FREE GIFT!

15 Don'ts and Dos

**Effectively Comfort
Your Hurting Friend**

A quick, but powerful
guide to give you some
immediate tools and
practical advice to help
be a comfort to a friend
who is struggling…
with any kind of loss.

- *Do you wish you knew how to be the right
  kind of friend when the worst things happen
  in their life?*

- *Do you feel clueless as to what to say when a
  friend loses a spouse or a child unexpectedly?*

- *Do you find it easier to step away from a
  friend's pain because you're fearful of adding
  to it?*

Then check out this **FREE PDF** to help you
overcome all this awkwardness!
You can grab your **FREE** copy here:

lynnehoeksema.com/15-donts-and-dos/

"Did you ever wish you had some sort of a handbook when you try to comfort a grieving loved one? Have you ever wished you had wisdom, so when you opened your mouth, words of encouragement would topple out? Lynne's book, *Cultivating Compassion* is just what you need. People have shared with me the hurtful things they were told while they were in grief. Others have cried from the loneliness they felt when their friends subtracted themselves from their lives. Having suffered through multiple losses in my life, I can attest that grieving is hard, impossible without God's help. Lynne knows this firsthand and did something about it. You will find yourself turning to her book again and again. And you'll probably want extra copies to give to others. Thank you, Lynne, for caring about those who are hurting. If you want to help someone who's grieving, you need this book."

-- Anne Peterson
Author of *Broken: A story of abuse, survival and hope* and *Droplets: Poetry for those in grief*

"Lynne has provided valuable wisdom to lawyers I've trained in mediation. Her insights into grief are applicable to clients facing divorce who grieve the changes in their family and losing time with their children."

-- Kimberly Stamatelos
Attorney, Mediator
Author of *The Compassionate Lawyer*

"As a former Hospice Director and recent widow myself, I can wholeheartedly confirm that what Lynne writes in her book is what we want our friends and support system to understand about our grief. We need you in our lives, now and down this long road; we want our pain and struggle to be acknowledged; we aren't looking for the perfect words from you, just listen as we process; let us grieve at our own pace. All the practical advice along with solid biblical support make this a 'go-to' book for anyone desiring to help their friend through any trial."

-- Kathy Davis
Hospice Director

"Small booklet, but extremely helpful! Through Lynne's journey in the unexpected loss of her dear husband, an extremely practical 'must read' booklet has been created. You will find this a help for all who are at a loss of what to say — or better yet, not to say — when a friend or loved one is experiencing a loss or going through a difficult time in life. I've seen, first-hand, how Lynne's faith has grown through this season of grieving, as she learns more of God's character and how He sanctifies through trials. That experience shines through in this booklet. I wish it had been given to me years ago. *Cultivating Compassion* has certainly prepared me to nurture others better in the future."

-- Gary Bock
Lead pastor, Timberline Church

CULTIVATING
COMPASSION

PRACTICAL ADVICE
AS YOU WALK A
FRIEND THROUGH
A SEASON OF LOSS

Lynne Hoeksema

Daisy Publishing
Urbandale, IA 50323
lynnehoeksema.com

Printed in the United States of America

Cover Design by Britney Wilson
Book Design by WORD**ART**, LLC West Des Moines, IA

Dedication

To my husband, Dale, whose love and support and encouragement throughout our life together helped mold me into the person I am today – a woman who misses you desperately, but who knows that God has called her to share all that she's learned in the process of losing you.

TABLE OF CONTENTS

Acknowledgments

To those instrumental in "launching" this ministry and this book: My pastor, Gary Bock, who said to me a few short months after Dale's death, "Lynne, I think you have a ministry here." To which I reluctantly responded, "I'm afraid you might be right!" And my friend, Renae Coddington, who said to me after my very first blog post, "You need to write a book." Of course, I said, "Oh no, that's not for me." Thank you for your unending encouragement throughout this journey!

To my ministry board of directors — Sue Koch, Angie Lookingbill, Susan Pfeil and Gary Higbee. You are the heart and the brains of my ministry and everything I do, including this book, is better because of your input.

To my faithful prayer team — your contribution often flies "under the radar," but I know how important each of you is to my success because I live the results of those prayers day in and day out. Thank you for being my prayer warriors!

Britney Wilson, you are an incredibly talented mixture of photographer and graphic designer, and everything looks more professional because of your hand upon it. Thank for your patience and kindness throughout.

To Karen Kehoe, my brilliant logo designer. Somehow you reached into this mathematical brain of mine and understood exactly what I was looking for, regardless of my meager attempts to describe it. You nailed it from the get-go!

Angie Lookingbill, you are so much more than just the dog mom of Daisy's best friend! Your willingness to use that editor's "red pencil" in such a kind and loving, but effective way helped take off the rough edges of this manuscript. Thank you for going the extra mile.

To my publishing guru, Bill Love, for your thoughtful and patient guidance through my first self-publishing venture. Your invaluable knowledge of the big picture allayed any fears I had about stepping into this world. And your meticulous attention to the interior design detail resulted in such a beautiful product.

To Anne Peterson, Kim Stamatelos, Kathy Davis, and Gary Bock for being willing to put your names next to mine. I'm grateful and humbled by your kind endorsements of my first publishing endeavor.

To my friends, too many to list here, for your encouragement, support, listening ears, ideas, prayers and so much more – I'm eternally grateful to have you all in my life.

And lastly, but most importantly, I'm grateful to God for all he continues to teach me about his character, his promises and his everlasting love for me. I'm a changed person through this season of life because of his sanctifying grace. This ministry is not only his gift to me; it *IS* his. He gives me the words to speak and to write, and I'm always in awe of how his care for me is shown through every detail of this ministry. To him be all praise and glory!

INTRODUCTION

When I landed on the title, *Cultivating Compassion*, several ideas came to mind that I want to share as you read through this, all focused on the word "cultivating." Coming from one of the top agricultural states in our nation, I can't help but think of the Spring planting season and the *CULTIVATING* that's necessary before those seeds go into the ground. Here's a brief definition that will serve us well:

> **Cultivating**: "Loosening and breaking up (tilling) of the soil. The soil around existing plants is cultivated (by hand using a hoe, or by machine using a cultivator) to destroy weeds and promote growth by increasing soil aeration and water infiltration. Soil being prepared for the planting of a crop is cultivated by a harrow or plow."

A more non-agricultural definition includes words like "foster," "nurture" and "encourage."

Some thoughts on how this applies to this subject of compassion:

- Some work is necessary *BEFORE* fruit is produced.

- Past misconceptions (weeds) may need to be removed for ideal growth.

- It's a process over time, not a "once and done" event.

- There is an element of caring throughout.

- There is an expectation of growth and fruit.

One of my favorite scripture verses sums this up very well — and reminds us that God is ultimately the One who can produce the best fruit in us.

> *So neither he who plants nor he who waters is anything, but only God who gives the growth* (1 Corinthians 3:7 ESV).

My journey, which resulted in this writing, began on Monday, October 16, 2017, the morning I received the phone call telling me that Dale, my husband of 31 years, had died.

Let me give you a bit of background.

I met Dale many years ago when we both worked for Northwestern Bell Telephone Company. He was 20 years older than me, had three grown children and, at the time, two grandchildren. Pretty much every parent's dream for their only daughter, right?! But, after dating for about five years, he did win over both of my parents, along with most of my family and friends. We married in 1986 on a big paddleboat on the Mississippi River out of the Port of Saint Paul.

Over the next 27 years, we were blessed to enjoy a great country life together, living on acreages in Minnesota and Iowa. I will forever be grateful for those years and the memories we made. But, as we all know, life isn't always a bed of roses, and 22 years into our marriage, in 2008, Dale was diagnosed with vascular dementia. He began to fail both mentally and physically, and eventually he couldn't do the work on the acreage and I couldn't do it alone. So, in 2013, we made the difficult decision to move into town.

His dementia worsened and by the end of 2016, I realized I couldn't keep him safe at home anymore and made another difficult decision to place him in an assisted living facility. Another blessing I'm so grateful for, is that during those last ten months, I could go from being the sole, full-time caregiver of someone with dementia to being his wife again. It was such an amazing time of restoration for our marriage after some difficult years. It became a time of reminiscing about our blessed life… a gift from God.

Despite the fact that I was "preparing" to lose him in the next year or so, I was completely blind-sided by the call I received that October morning telling me Dale had passed away. The next days and weeks were filled with all that becoming a widow entails, the visitation and funeral planning, going through his clothes, cancelling credit cards, changing the names on our utilities and a multitude of other "to-do list" type activities.

But the truly hard work was grieving the loss of this man that I had loved for most of my adult life. The pain was deep, visceral, powerful and relentless. I wouldn't wish it on anyone. Having already lost both of my parents,

I can safely say that it's the hardest thing I will ever go through in my life. And I'm still going through it — probably forever, to some degree.

Once the initial rush associated with the visitation and funeral was over, I began to sense that some of my friends were uncomfortable around me. They clearly didn't know what to do or say, and that discomfort ultimately led to a change in many friendships. As I talked with other widows or read blog posts and articles on the subject, I found that it was a common phenomenon. When they lost their husband, they lost friends.

The fear of doing or saying the wrong thing ultimately led to friends distancing themselves from me or disappearing from my life. And, unfortunately, it came at a time when I could least afford additional heartache.

But here's the thing — I could relate to how they felt! That's right. I had been on that side of someone's grief and pain as well. For much of my life, I, too, had no idea what to do or say. I *KNOW* I didn't always step in and be a comfort to friends when they were going through a tough time.

So, this is *NOT* written from a perspective

of judgment. It's a result of a clear calling to shed some light on this difficult topic. It is intended to help you understand what it's like to be on this side of a painful loss and provide some insight and practical advice that can ultimately help you be a blessing to your hurting friend.

I want it to be full of "aha" moments for you. I want it to be full of ways you have never looked at loss before and full of words you never realized could be unintentionally hurtful. I want you to see why listening is one of the most powerful gifts you can give your friend. I want to give you practical advice and the "whys" behind it to give you the confidence and compassion you need to step into your friend's pain — and ultimately see blessings for both of you.

Even though I speak from the perspective of widowhood, I have found that the principles I share with you can be applied to nearly any kind of loss that someone is experiencing — and how you interact with them. Of course, loss from death is automatically included in that list. Spouse, child, miscarriage, parent, grandparent, sibling, friend, even our beloved pets. But what about other kinds of losses? What about job loss, or disability, or divorce, or cancer or chronic illness? Or any other way that we can suffer in this fallen world? I hope that what I share with you can equip you to help someone regardless of why they're suffering.

My prayer is that, through this booklet, you'll receive tools for your compassion arsenal to help you walk confidently alongside that hurting friend.

CHAPTER 1

IS THIS FOR YOU?

Thank you for picking up this booklet! That act alone shows that you have a heart for someone who is hurting - or at least a curiosity as to how you can best help your friend.

Unlike so many resources on the market today, this is NOT for the people who are grieving a death or loss. There are books, blogs, articles and grief support groups all geared specifically for the person feeling the loss the deepest.

The purpose of this booklet is to provide one more critical resource for that grieving person. YOU! That's right, this is for those of you who comprise their support system. And don't think that you have to be in the circle of "best friends" to be a comfort.

A neighbor that I knew primarily through our dogs, stopped by the first Valentine's Day after my husband died to give me flowers. She said, "I thought Dale would want you to have these." I can't tell you how powerful that was — and what a huge blessing it was to me on a very difficult day.

What are the names of the people who came to mind when you received this book? Regardless of whether they are a best friend or an acquaintance, you are likely in the circle of influence that can minister comfort to them.

Let's face it, stepping into someone's pain with them is awkward and uncomfortable. Often, we just don't know what to do with them! And that feeling is widespread. Have you ever thought or said any these things?

- I have no idea what to say to him/her.

- I don't want to say the wrong thing.

- I'm afraid I'll make him/her cry.

- I'm afraid *I'll* cry.

- I don't want to make things worse.

- I don't want to bring "it" up.

- I'm not really a nurturer.

- I don't have the gift of compassion.

If you answered "yes" to any of these, I guarantee you are in good company! Few people feel comfortable knowing what to say or do in these circumstances and the result is that we often just disappear, hoping that they won't notice our absence.

I can tell you it doesn't go unnoticed. And it adds more heartache at a time when the grieving person can least afford to take that on.

So, if you could learn, in the comfort of your own home, some simple but powerful concepts that would give you the tools and confidence to step into that hurting friend's life, would you welcome the opportunity?

That's exactly the intention of this book. To give you the resources — and the motivation — for stepping into someone's pain with them, and ultimately being a blessing during their difficult days.

And here are a couple of bonuses:

- You will also be blessed in the process.

- Your relationship with your friend can grow richer and deeper.

- These techniques and suggestions can be used to help someone going through any kind of trial – not just loss from death.

So, let's get started.

CHAPTER 2

WHAT IS YOUR FRIEND EXPERIENCING?

You may already have some insights as to what your grieving friend is experiencing. Maybe you've been through a similar loss. Maybe you've been through a devastating loss. Or maybe you've just been an observer, looking in from the outside.

Regardless of your experience, this friend's journey is absolutely unique. No one knows exactly what they are going through. We'll discuss the risks of making comparisons in Chapter 11. For now, just be aware that this unique journey will likely exhibit a full array of emotions and reactions.

And if you've never gone through a truly

deep loss, this will help broaden your perspectives on grieving and give you a start on building compassion. Because, I do believe it's vitally important to have some sense of what they are experiencing, even if you don't fully understand it. Just know that any of these emotions can be true for your grieving friend. And accept them without judgment.

This is by no means an all-inclusive list, but these are often emotions that they'll struggle with during the early days and months of loss.

Shock/Denial

Of course, this emotion will be front and center if the death was sudden or tragic. But, knowing that someone is dying does *NOT* eliminate the shock. The finality of the death can still trigger this emotion, regardless of how much "warning" you have. So, don't be "shocked" when you see this in your friend. You may even see some evidence of denial along with this shock. A death can absolutely rock their world, and denial is often a defense mechanism to hold some of that pain at bay.

Sadness/Depression

This may seem so obvious that it doesn't warrant a listing here, but I want to remind you that deep, gut-wrenching sorrow may be a constant companion to your grieving friend. Yes, it may lessen a bit over time, but it's also possible that your friend has learned to hide that aspect in public. In the privacy of their own home, it may look much different. Knowing when sadness morphs into clinical depression is tricky, so consult a professional if you think your friend may become suicidal.

Confusion

The stress of working through a loss can wreak havoc on our normal brain functions resulting in very muddled thinking. And this can go on for months. There's even a phenomenon known as "widow's fog!" Without going into all the scientific support behind this, just know that it can be incredibly difficult to focus on anything in the months following a loss. Often, it's just a matter of going through the motions. Disorganization and forgetfulness may abound. Have grace!

Anger

Anger can be directed in so many ways and some may make no sense to you as the observer. They may be angry at the person who died, or angry at someone who was their caregiver. Maybe they're angry with themselves, feeling that they didn't do "enough." They could be angry at God. It's a common emotion after a loss and is part of the grieving process. Let them feel what they're feeling. And worth repeating, reserve judgment.

Guilt

Often a companion emotion to anger, they may be overcome with guilt on many levels. Maybe they wish they could have done more before their loved one died. Maybe they're dredging up all the times they said or did something they wish they could take back or redo now. Some may even experience guilt over the relief they are feeling that the loved one's suffering is over. Or, if a relationship was rocky or complicated, they may even feel guilty that they aren't grieving more deeply.

Fear/Anxiety

Something many of us experience in life is the fear of the unknown. It can certainly lead to some anxious days and nights. So, it's no surprise if these emotions loom large in the life of the grieving friend. At a minimum, everyone who grieves can be fearful that they may never feel normal again, or ever be happy again. Add to that the fear of what life now looks like without their loved one and it can become overwhelming. All of these areas can be affected by this loss – finances, daily routine, social status, living conditions, faith, family dynamics, circle of friends and many more.

This brief overview can't do justice to all the nuances that a grieving person will experience. Just know that everyone's journey is unique. Don't be surprised by unusual behaviors. And be cautious about minimizing their feelings and emotions. In short, have grace and reserve judgment!

CHAPTER 3

WHAT IS YOUR MOTIVATION?

Because stepping into a friend's pain can be so difficult and uncomfortable, it's important to touch on the subject of motivation. Just what causes you to overcome those awkward feelings and take the step toward your hurting friend?

Gift of Compassion

I think it's safe to say that some people do seem to have a heart to walk alongside those who are hurting. Maybe their own heartaches and trials have given them this rare perspective. If you're one of those people, be grateful that you can use your past or present pain to help someone else along that path. Others have personalities that draw them to the needs of others.

But, in my experience, this is *NOT* the norm. So, if you feel that you aren't a nurturer or don't have the gift of compassion, there is still hope for you. Just keep reading!

It's the Right Thing to Do

Maybe your motivation for stepping into your friend's hurting world is simply because you know it's the right thing to do. You may or may not have all the tools, but you inherently know that they need you during these dark days. So, you've put your discomfort aside to focus on how you can minister to them when they need you most. If this describes you, my hat is off to you! Keep up the good work. These friends often say things like, "I have no idea what to say to you, but I'm here." That can often be enough.

Spiritual Motivation

If you are a Christian, your motivation very simply can be because God's Word, the Bible, exhorts us to be people of compassion. There are many scripture texts that call us to this kind of service. I want to do justice to this topic, so I expound on how God can equip us for this ministry in Appendix A. It's one of my favorite areas to discuss and a couple of paragraphs can barely scratch that surface. We'll take a look at some key scripture texts that show us not only why it's important to be compassionate, but also *HOW* God's Spirit can equip us for this important mission.

Regardless of what spurs you on, please consider putting your discomfort aside and focusing on the pain your friend is experiencing. The motivation to continue walking alongside them may come as you take small action steps and witness the power of compassion.

CHAPTER 4

I NEED HELP NOW!

Those first few days after the loss of a loved one can be an absolute flurry of activity, especially if the death was sudden. So many details to take care of just to get the visitation and funeral planned. Add to that, family or friends coming into town, perhaps purchasing a cemetery plot, or helping other family members process the loss. The list can be endless.

Most of us do a pretty decent job of being present in a grieving friend's life during these first days. Maybe you've stopped by with a casserole, or a grocery bag full of paper products (including toilet paper!) or just to give them a hug and have a cry with them. These are all good steps and certainly much appreciated.

On the day of the visitation or funeral, offer to watch pets, children or even the house. Sadly, thieves are checking obituaries to see when a family will be away from their home so that they can break in and add more chaos to their lives.

Your presence at a visitation or funeral can be a huge comfort for your hurting friend. I found it strangely heartening to simply read through the signatures of those who attended my husband's.

What are some other practical ways to reach out in those early days? Of course, it varies depending on whom they've lost. I would also suggest getting some sort of approval before barging in and taking over their lives as there are some areas they may not want help with. So, with those caveats, here are some suggestions:

- Take the children to the park or a movie.

- Invite them over for a meal – or deliver a meal past those first few days.

- Help organize paperwork after the death. There's a *LOT* to be done.

- Write thank-yous for or with them.

- Make phone calls to utilities, insurance companies, credit card companies, etc.

- Go through the loved one's clothing or other belongings with them (be cautious as this can be very personal).

- Take them out to the spa or a sporting event.

- Mow the lawn; shovel the driveway.

- Remember the extra difficult days like holidays, birthdays, anniversaries — especially if they follow shortly after the death.

- *ASK THEM* what would be most helpful to them — they might surprise you with something you never even considered doing.

This is really just a sampling of the ways you can be a blessing in those early days after the loss. Need more ideas? Google is a huge resource!

The important message here is to still be present in the days and weeks after the visitation and funeral. The surface of their grief has barely been scratched. Don't be the friend who disappears.

CHAPTER 5

TEARS!

This is the perfect transition topic between immediate helps and long-term helps. Because the person who's grieving may be crying from Day One until forever.

So, let's talk about the basics of tears.

Have you ever experienced what it means to "have a good cry?" Sometimes we feel so much better after we've done that, don't we? But there is science behind that phenomenon and it's pretty incredible. Scientists have analyzed the physiological make-up of onion-peeling tears and emotional tears. They are different!

There are toxins in the emotional tears that aren't present in those onion-peeling ones.

That's because the toxins are being cleansed from our bodies *THROUGH* our emotional tears. Isn't that amazing? We are created to heal through our tears.

So, what should that tell us? It's okay to cry! Crying should be encouraged! Not just for the person who's grieving, but for anyone who cares about them. Cry with your friend. It's a bond like no other.

Somehow our society has associated tears with weakness, especially for the male gender. But bottling emotions inside can often result in unhealthy or destructive behaviors somewhere down the line.

What do the grieving person's tears reflect? Simply put, they are a direct reflection of their love for the one who died. They show the depth of sorrow and sense of loss they're experiencing. What could make more sense or be more natural than that?

The tears you shed *WITH* them have meaning as well. They demonstrate your willingness to be vulnerable with them. They acknowledge that you understand the depth of their loss, and that can mean the world to them.

So, how should you react to their tears?

- Worth repeating — yes, you may cry with them!

- Give them a hug.

- Wait while they cry — and then let them talk.

- Remind them that you still hurt for them, you're still praying for them.

- *DON'T* apologize if you think you caused it. Remember, you're helping them heal.

- *DON'T* back away when their tears start. They can likely sense that immediately and it's hurtful.

CHAPTER 6

TRIALS

The purpose of this short chapter is to simply touch on the reality that everyone goes through trials at some point in their life. Some trials are more like minor irritations — others are devastating. The death of a loved one is much closer to the devastating end of the scale.

One can find many clichés about trials, especially in the world of motivational speaking. And stories abound chronicling how someone rose from the ashes of their trial to go on to do great things.

There can be much truth here and many lessons to learn, and I personally feel that the trials we endure can give us a strength and character we would never have attained without them.

I feel so strongly about this that I have included Appendix B at the end to take a biblical look at the role trials play in our lives.

My caution for you, the friend comforter, is this: Please avoid any statements that minimize your friend's pain by suggesting that this trial will make them stronger in the end. While that may eventually be true, your suggestion will certainly not make it a reality, and it could be so far out on their horizon as to be irrelevant to them today.

CHAPTER 7

GRIEF ACKNOWLEDGMENT

I'd like to introduce two overarching principles in the world of being a comforter that can hopefully give you a framework under which all else will fall. In other words, the things you should and shouldn't say, and the things you should and shouldn't do, can all be directly determined by how well you understand the concepts behind these two principles.

The first is "*Grief Acknowledgment*." Simply put, it's acknowledging their pain. Acknowledging that this may be a difficult season for your friend. Acknowledging that *THIS* may be the hardest thing they've ever gone through.

Front and center under this principle, and

critical to being an effective comforter, is getting a grasp on how long their grieving may last — and how deep it may be. I use the word "*grasp*" because I don't believe it's necessary — or possible — to know exactly what the grieving person is going through.

In my experience, it's more powerful and comforting to have a friend who doesn't question the way I'm grieving or if I'm *STILL* grieving. To accept it without judgment is a tremendous gift. Much of the practical advice I share in subsequent chapters is based on this very premise.

So, having that mentality firmly in place will serve you and your friend well, as you step into this loss with them.

Here's the truth about how long we grieve. It takes as long as it takes. Sorry I can't give you something more profound — or helpful. But this is the truth. The depth of the relationship, the manner of death and a multitude of other factors can certainly affect the length of one's grief.

I grieved the death of each of my parents differently, and for different lengths of time. I was very close to both parents, but my dad died very unexpectedly at a younger age and my mom died after wasting away from dementia.

Today, decades after their deaths, I still miss them and can still occasionally shed tears, but I don't grieve their losses daily.

The death of my husband? Completely different story. As of this writing, I'm about 18 months into this life-changing loss, and the grief is only getting worse. And sadly, that is the norm according to the scores of people I've talked with and the articles and blog posts I've read.

Whether you understand it or agree with it, I believe this statement to be true — some grieving is forever. Some losses forever change us. That's how I feel about the loss of my husband of 31 years.

It's how my friends who have lost a child feel. They are forever changed by their loss. There's a reason that *"Death of spouse/death of child"* are at the very top of the *"Life Stressors"* lists. They are *LIFE-ALTERING* events. That doesn't mean for a few weeks or months. It means for the rest of their lives. Take a moment to let the reality of that sink in if this is a new concept to you. It can change the lens through which you view your friend and their grief.

Acknowledging that your friend may be

grieving long after the actual loss is absolutely key. One of the worst things you can do when a friend experiences a deep loss is... *nothing*! I'll share some suggestions on what words are helpful and which ones aren't in a later chapter, but I want to make this point crystal clear:

> **Acknowledgment of their pain and grief— for as long as it takes — is one of the most important and comforting things you can do for your hurting friend.**

CHAPTER 8

QUICK-FIX-IT MENTALITY

The second overarching principle is the *"Quick-Fix-It Mentality."* We live in a society today that isn't comfortable around unhappiness, brokenness, pain, heartache or anything that makes us feel awkward. If you doubt this, just check out all the self-help books on the shelf or on Amazon. Listen to a handful of daytime talk shows. Even many sermons from the pulpits today are geared towards "fixing" anything that might be making you less than what you could or should be.

Granted, there are times when moving someone toward a happier or healthier existence is appropriate. But this is definitely not a one-size-fits-all solution. And your discomfort should not be what drives this. So, the heart of this principle is realizing that the best way to comfort your grieving friend is to *AVOID* this quick-fix-it mentality when it comes to their grief. Just check your own timetable for their grief at the door, and have zero expectations on when they should "move on." Often someone's emotions don't fully surface until months or even years after their loss.

This is a tough one. It *IS* hard to be around someone who is grieving. It's true that some people try to rush their friends through the grieving process because it makes *THEM* uncomfortable. A wise widow friend told me early on, "Lynne, people want you to get over this quickly, so that *THEY* can feel better!" I know, it's a little bit funny — but a little bit true.

But it's just as true that you simply don't want your friend to hurt. We want to take away their pain because we love them and want their life to be joy-filled again.

So, I want to extend grace in this chapter and not beat anyone up for desiring a *"sooner the better,"* pain-free life for your friend.

But the reality is what we just discussed in the previous chapter. Sometimes it takes a *LONG* time to process a loss. And moving someone through it too quickly can add to their struggles. We'll look at this in more detail in Chapter 11 when I share some specific cautions.

A grieving person is often extremely fragile. This particular loss might be either their first experience with it — or it might be the deepest loss they've ever gone through. In both circumstances, they probably have no idea how to handle it or what it should look like. They may question if they are normal, or if they are processing their grief "properly." Any indication from their friends that they aren't doing this correctly, even if it's unintentional, can add to their heartache.

Is this starting to feel like it's out of your control? That's probably a good sign! Because, the reality is that it IS out of your control. You can't affect how your friend grieves, for how long or how deep. You can't fix it and you can't take their pain away. The hard work of grieving is primarily done alone.

But that doesn't mean you have nothing in your compassion arsenal. The next chapter addresses one of the most comforting and powerful gifts you can give to your grieving friend.

CHAPTER 9

LISTENING

Are you surprised that one of the most comforting things you can do for your friend requires very few words from you? Are you secretly relieved? One of the fears so many of us have when dealing with a grieving friend is that of saying the wrong thing. And I will address things to say and not to say soon, but for now I want you to grasp the importance of the fine art of listening.

I can best illustrate this with a story from my own early days of grieving. A few days after my husband's funeral, a friend, who had never met Dale and only knew me during the days of his dementia called me up and said, "Lynne, I'd like to find a time to come over and just let you tell me about this wonderful man."

WOW! That's exactly what I needed! Even if I didn't know it. If I could give you a sample of what it means to be a comfort to your hurting friend, this would be it. Do you see how simple that is? Do you see how there was no attempt to fix the pain, or move me through my grief? Do you see how this friend took herself completely out of the picture and consequently didn't have to struggle with the "right words?"

Maybe you're also surprised (appalled?) that she brought up my loved one. Do you think you'll remind us of our loss by bringing it up? It's not true. There's no way we've forgotten about them. Seriously, it's there all the time.

But what I most wanted to talk about was my life with Dale — what I loved about him, my memories of our life together and the kind of person he was. I can't understate or undervalue the healing power of talking about him. And to have my friend sit and listen to this for hours was a gift beyond measure.

If you knew their loved one, let them know what you most appreciated about them. Or tell them a story that highlights one of their loved one's best characteristics. It's okay if the story makes them laugh… or cry. As irrational as this sounds, we are often fearful that our loved one will be forgotten, so you can keep them alive in our memories by sharing these stories.

And for goodness sake, use the loved one's name. Yes, it really is okay. It's almost like music to our ears. It's one way to show that you're in this with them, that you're not afraid to say their name and see where that conversation takes you.

Maybe it's their loved one they want to talk about. But there are other things that may be helpful for them to talk through as well. Maybe they want to talk about *HOW* their loved one died. I know that may seem strange, but it's pretty common to need to process that as well. Maybe they need to talk about their regrets. We all have them. Perhaps it's their anger or fear or shock or any other emotion they're struggling with. Maybe it's the tasks that lie ahead of them, and how overwhelmed they feel by that.

Regardless of *WHAT* they want to talk through, it's vitally important that you listen without judgment. Don't minimize their feelings by telling them they shouldn't feel that way, or trying to come up with a "fix." We *DO* feel that way! Just let us.

Let them cry. Cry with them. Don't feel the need to fill up the silence with your words. That can often lead to unhelpful platitudes which may only serve to hurt them further. Chapter 12 looks at this in greater detail.

So, the words that *ARE* important in this chapter are the questions you ask them to begin the conversation. And the follow-up questions you ask as the conversation progresses, with the focus squarely on your friend and their pain. Or the stories you share about their loved one. Powerful and healing words.

CHAPTER 10

THE "RIGHT WORDS"

First of all, let me stress once more the importance of listening as outlined in the previous chapter. But sometimes, it *DOES* take a few words from you to get the conversation started so that you can listen to their heart. Sometimes these may be over the phone. If possible, and your friend has the time, it can be more powerful and helpful in person. Here are a few suggestions on how to start that conversation:

- Tell me about _____ (*their loved one's name – if you didn't know them*).

- This is what I most appreciated about _____.

- One of my favorite things about
  _____ was _____.

- This is one of my favorite stories about
  _____.

- I remember when _____.

- Tell me about (*the day they passed away*).

- What happened? (**Note**: *Very simple, but effective when you learn of a sudden loss in a friend's life. Continue to ask follow-up questions as they tell you the story.*)

- What are your favorite memories?

- What are you missing the most?

- What do you most need prayer for?

- What are your immediate needs?

We talked in Chapter 7 about acknowledging their grief. This is important from the moment you first learn of their loss until long after the funeral service or the onset of the crisis. Consequently, these next suggestions which *DO* acknowledge that grief, can be used for months after the loss.

It might be helpful for you to think through these next statements with that in mind. Obviously, they are appropriate when you first talk with your friend, whether it be at their home, over the phone, or at the visitation or funeral. They could even be the words you use through email, text, FaceBook or cards in the mail.

But, more importantly — and more rarely — these can and should be used for months and sometimes even years after the loss. Because if you buy into the notion we discussed earlier about some grieving lasting forever, these statements can bring a sense of comfort no matter how much time has passed. If there is still deep grief in your friend's life, these words are appropriate.

Here are some suggestions for those "grief-acknowledgement" conversations:

- I am so sorry you're going through this.

- I don't even know what to say to you, but I'm here.

- I'm just calling to call.

- I can't imagine how hard this is.

- My heart hurts for you.

- How can I pray for you?

- I'm here for you for the long haul.

- You must be feeling completely over-whelmed right now.

- I'm so sorry for your pain.

It's important that your conversation feels natural and sounds like "you." It shouldn't be the memorization of this list — it's just a few suggestions. Speak from your heart.

And remember, the heart from which you speak *IS* more important than the words you say. So don't be afraid to let that heart shine through when you're talking with your friend — even shedding a few tears with them. I could always sense when my friends' hearts truly did hurt for me — and that surpassed any words they might have shared with me.

CHAPTER 11

WORDS OF CAUTION

I almost feel like apologizing ahead of time for the length of this chapter compared to that of the previous one! But I guess it shouldn't be that surprising if we understand the priority of listening over having the right words.

That said, many times words said out of good intentions can actually be hurtful to the grieving person if you've never walked in the shoes of deep grief. Or if your journey was quite different. So this is certainly not an all-inclusive list, nor is it a list of words you should never say. My goal here is to provide some perspective on how the *POSSIBILITY* of hurt lies within these statements.

So, rather than giving you a simple list as I did in previous chapters, I want to offer a little background for you which can hopefully provide the perspective necessary to see these statements as the grieving person may.

"Let me know if you need anything."

Haven't we all said this? I know I certainly have — many times, and I *STILL* catch myself saying it. Of course, I meant it. Because, how can we know how to help the grieving person if they don't tell us, right?

Well, here's the reality of my world after Dale's death. I heard these statements often:

- *If you want to go to coffee sometime, let me know.*

- *If you want to go to dinner, let me know.*

- *If you want to catch a movie sometime, let me know.*

- *If you want to go for a walk, let me know.*

- *IF YOU NEED ANYTHING... let me know.*

Did you get a sense, even in the listing of these statements, how that might feel to the grieving person? I heard those statements a lot — sometimes from almost everyone I talked within a day. And, even acknowledging that they had the best of intentions, it was overwhelming to me.

Reality? I absolutely did not have the strength to reach out. Sometimes it was all I could do to get out of bed in the morning. Good thing I had a couple of dogs that needed to be let out…

So, what do you do instead?

Be the person who says, "Let's set a date to go to dinner/coffee/a walk/a movie etc…" And then *ALSO* be the person who understands if they just can't do it yet. But don't give up on them.

I often found it more comfortable to meet with my friends at my house over take-out meals. That way my emotions weren't on display in a very public place. We could talk freely about this loss and not be restricted by the surroundings.

"I know [exactly] how you feel. I felt like that when…"

No, you don't! Even if you've been through a similar loss, *EVERYONE'S* journey is unique. You may feel, as I often did before Dale's death, that you're helping them feel less alone by relating to them on this level. Again, good intentions, but here's how that can go wrong:

1. You just shifted the focus from their deep, *IMMEDIATE* pain to your past pain. I didn't have the capacity to take on anyone else's pain at that point.

2. You take away the unique nature of *MY* pain. No one knew what it was like to love this man for more than 35 years, watch dementia steal away much of our joy and then experience the shock of receiving that fateful phone call, "He passed." No one has our history and to assume you can understand it exactly is hurtful. I don't need you to fully understand my pain to be a comfort to me.

3. You run the risk of minimizing their loss if the comparison you just made rings pretty hollow to them. Soon after my husband's funeral, someone told me they knew exactly how I felt because they felt like that when they went through their divorce. Nope, not the same thing! I don't know how it felt to go through their divorce either. The comment might *SOUND* like this to us —"I know exactly how you feel. I felt like that when my goldfish died." Yep, not helpful...

If we think about this logically, it does make sense that we can't know how someone feels in their grief. Think of all that goes into making you who you are today. Add to that all that went into making your loved one who they are. And then add all the nuances of your relationship with them. Put that together, along with the individual circumstances of their death and your response to it, and it equals — *UNIQUE JOURNEY*. When you lose that loved one, no one has more than a glimpse into what it feels like to you. God was the only one who knew exactly how I felt.

"Well, at least…"

Even without knowing what the rest of that sentence is, you might see how that statement could also minimize the grieving friend's pain. "You really shouldn't feel so bad because at least you have… *THIS*." I guarantee that won't make them more appreciative!

Some of these statements can seem comforting and even truthful. For example:

"At least they didn't suffer."

"At least their suffering is over."

"At least they're in heaven."

"At least you could be there with them."

In my experience, it was better for me to arrive at these statements on my own, rather than have someone use them to try to make me feel better than I did, to move me through my pain too quickly.

And here's a risk you run — sometimes those statements can take you down a very wrong road. I have a friend who lost her son in a car accident many years ago and someone said to her at the time, "Well, at least you still have your daughter." Do you think that gave her any comfort? Nope. So be safe and don't even start a sentence with, "Well, at least..."

"You [just] need to...

...get out more."

...see a doctor about some medication."

...stop being so angry/sad/depressed."

...start dating."

...start eating more."

...start eating less." (*Yikes!*)

If you find yourself using these statements, maybe you've inadvertently stepped into the doctor/therapist role. That's likely *NOT* what your friend needs. They may very well utilize the skills of a doctor or counselor at some point on their journey, but that's not what I needed from my friends.

And when you add the "just" to any of those statements, it sounds like we "just" need to make this one little adjustment and our grieving will be over. Who knew it was that simple!?

One caveat in this discussion worth mentioning again: If you are walking alongside a friend who starts to exhibit some alarming behavior, or you're afraid they might harm themselves, don't take chances with that. Contact a professional to help you navigate this situation.

CHAPTER 12

PLATITUDES AND SCRIPTURE

It's not unusual to rely on some common platitudes when trying to provide comfort to your friend. But so often these are not helpful. At the very least, they ring hollow. Some are biblically inaccurate. Sometimes they just make us feel worse because we feel like we aren't grieving properly or fast enough. They all have one thing in common. The intent is to make us feel better...and sooner. But it has to take whatever time it takes. Here are some examples:

> "God needed your loved one more than you did."

"God needed another angel."

"Your loved one wouldn't want you to be sad."

"Your loved one would want you to move on."

"Be strong — that's what they'd want."

In earlier chapters, we discussed the two main principles of *Grief Acknowledgment* and avoiding a *Quick-Fix-It Mentality*. I believe you can see how one or both of those concepts is lacking in these statements.

What about sharing scripture? If you and your friend are Christians, you may very well feel that scripture sharing would be helpful. And sometimes — and some *DAY* — it might be.

But sharing the scripture about how "all things work together for good..." may do more harm than good if you share that with someone who's just been dealt a devastating blow. And they may not want to hear about how this heartbreaking loss was God's will.

I would encourage caution and discernment in this area.

As with the sharing of platitudes, I found

that the scripture God led me to during my own quiet time or devotions was much more comforting and relevant than the scripture someone was using to try to fix me or move me past my pain.

CHAPTER 13

REACHING OUT

In Chapter 4, we discussed some ways to reach out to your friend in the early days after their loss. And, as a general rule, I think most of us are more comfortable in those times. We can express our condolences and drop off our casseroles without too much uneasiness.

But what about reaching out weeks, months or even years after the loss? That's the time when most people get back to their own lives and often make no effort to check in with their friends. But I can tell you emphatically that these are the days when we *MOST* need our friends.

Grief often gets much deeper and more

visceral as time goes by. The second year of widowhood is notoriously worse than the first year. So, if you are looking for a fail-proof way of being a comfort to your friend, don't disappear after the funeral.

I can't understate the power of your text, email, FaceBook message, phone call or note in the mail, letting them know that you're thinking of them or praying for them. Even a FaceBook "like" on one of their sentimental posts is a good thing. The manner really doesn't matter. It's the doing of it that matters the most.

Checking in with your friend on those extra hard days can be a huge comfort. Maybe it's a birthday or anniversary. Mother's Day or Father's Day can be extremely painful. Holidays are especially difficult days. And of course, the anniversary of the loved one's death — and the days leading up to it — can often cause the griever to relive the days surrounding the death.

Consider inviting them to go with you to an event that may be difficult for them to do alone. Even the first day back to church alone can cause high anxiety. Perhaps it's a baby shower, wedding or funeral. Any one of those may conjure up extra painful memories.

So, just what do you say to them when you're reaching out? Here are some suggestions:

"How are you doing? "

"How did your day go?"

"What are you feeling today?"

"How is the journey?"

"What are your immediate prayer needs."

"Do you need to talk?"

"Was there anything especially difficult in your day?"

Do you see how any one of these serves to help your grieving friend process their pain? If they choose to talk about it, your role is to listen without judgment and without advice, unless requested.

You can also use many of the grief acknowledgment statements we looked at in Chapter 10. I don't think there's an expiration date on saying, "I'm so sorry you're going through this." Or "My heart [still] hurts for you." Or "I am [still] praying for you."

Grief acknowledgment isn't just for the

few weeks after the loss; it can be a forever gift
to your friend.

CHAPTER 14

FINAL WORDS

First, some miscellaneous pieces of advice.

What if the suggestions I've given you here don't seem to fit your friend's situation? What if the grieving person doesn't seem to want or need you in their life? That's very possible because everyone does grieve differently.

Maybe they are finding other ways to process their grief. It could be with their family members, or a counselor or another friend. Maybe they aren't ready to deal with their grief yet. So, in both cases, I think it's okay to back off a bit, but also wise to stay on the periphery of their lives, because maybe they will need you somewhere down the line.

In Chapter 1, we looked at some of the reasons we don't reach out to people. And most were associated with some discomfort on our parts. But there are often real legitimate reasons why someone doesn't reach out.

You may have suffered a major loss in your own life, either recently or in the past, and you haven't processed that yet. You may be dealing with a crisis in your own life, big or small, or in the life of a loved one and you have nothing left in your tank. Your friend's loss might remind you of what's ahead for you, and you aren't prepared to face that yet.

So be kind to yourself. Becoming that person of compassion doesn't happen overnight. Take baby steps. Start with a FaceBook "like" and eventually move up to that face-to-face "how are you doing" conversation!

And finally, if you haven't been the friend you wanted to be, is it ever too late to apologize and step back into their life? I would say, no. I've learned that it's important for me to have grace in this process, and acknowledge that it's uncomfortable for so many. So, if someone apologizes for not being there for me, and wants to now be more supportive and connected, that's a very good thing. I want them back in my life.

I also don't think it's ever too late to send that sympathy card. I received cards many weeks after my husband's death and they were all precious to me.

So, if a few months have passed since your friend's loss, you could write something like this in that sympathy card:

> "I'm so sorry that I haven't sent this
> sooner. [*Period. No excuses.*] I haven't
> been the friend you needed and, for that,
> I want to apologize. I'm praying for
> you... [*whatever you deem appropriate*]."

And, if you really do want to reconnect, mention that you will call / send a message soon to get together. Don't say, "If you want to get together sometime, let me know." Remember, grieving people often don't have the strength to do the reaching out.

So, what are the main take-aways from this booklet?

- Don't disappear — Do something, no matter how small, or how long after the loss was suffered. Do something to show you care.

- Have a listening ear, rather than stressing over the right words.

- And remember the two main principles:

  o Avoid the quick-fix-it mentality by letting them grieve as long as they need.

  o Acknowledge their grief — acknowledge their pain rather than trying to fix it, or stepping out of their life because you can't!

Thank you so much for taking the time to read through this booklet! The fact that you've reached the end shows that you DO have a heart to help your hurting friend. I hope this has challenged you with some new perspectives and given you some practical advice that will help you step into your hurting friend's life when they need you. You will BOTH be blessed when you do.

Appendix A

What Does The Bible Say About Compassion?

Let's take a deeper look into God's Word to see what it teaches us about being compassionate and especially what we can learn about how God equips us.

As Christians, we have resources available to us that can make our witness extremely effective. First of all, we have God's Word to show us what kindness looks like and why it's so necessary. *AND*, we have the secret weapon of the Holy Spirit.

Because so few people feel comfortable stepping into someone's pain, it creates what I call a huge compassion gap. So when we, as believers, tap into these resources from God, we can step into that compassion gap and fill it with love and kindness. We *CAN* be the hands and feet of Jesus in this hurting world and, in the process, be a powerful witness for the Gospel.

Just what does the Bible say about compassion? Actually, it says a *LOT* about it — and that, in and of itself, should tell us that it's an important concept for God's Church to embrace.

My goal here is not to provide an exhaustive review of all those verses. But there are a few key texts that I believe give us a good foundation for what we're trying to learn.

Let's start by looking at God's heart.

In Psalm 68:5, it says:

Father to the fatherless and defender of widows is God in His holy habitation.

The orphan and the widow were often singled out as two groups needing extra protection in the Bible and God is the primary source of that protection. So, he knows how critically necessary this compassion is. Yes, he *IS* the Great Comforter.

What does the Bible tell us about Jesus' heart? If you know your New Testament Bible stories at all, you know that Jesus had such a heart of compassion for the hurting and the lonely and the disabled and the lost. As in everything, Jesus' life on this earth is the perfect example of what we should strive for.

I think this is shown in such a powerful way when Jesus was dying on the cross. In John 19:26-27 we read:

When Jesus saw his mother and the disciple whom he loved [this was John] standing nearby, he said to his mother, "Woman, behold, your son!" Then he said to the disciple, "Behold, your mother!" And from that hour the disciple took her to his own home.

So even when Jesus was dying, he made sure that his widowed mother was cared for. Such a tender picture of compassion!

But what about us mere mortals? What does the Bible offer up to us? Let's look at a couple of texts that give us some guidance in this area.

In this text from James 2:15-16 we read:

If a brother or sister is poorly clothed and lacking in daily food, and one of you says to them, "Go in peace, be warmed and filled," without giving them the things needed for the body, what good is that?

I have often tried to ease my guilt of *NOT* reaching out to someone who was hurting, by reminding myself that I *WAS* praying for them. And please don't misunderstand me, prayer is necessary; it's powerful, it's God-ordained, it's effective, so please don't stop praying.

But James is *ALSO* calling us to action in this text. Don't *JUST* pray for someone to be warm and filled. Give them food and a warm blanket. Don't *JUST* pray that God would raise up someone to take your grieving friend to coffee. BE the person who invites them. Yes, pray. But then move from your prayer closet out into the streets.

Another text with great instruction for us comes in 2 Corinthians 1:3-4, where we read:

> *Blessed be the God and Father of our Lord Jesus Christ, the Father of mercies and God of all comfort, who comforts us in all our affliction, so that we may be able to comfort those who are in any affliction, with the comfort with which we ourselves are comforted by God.*

I'd like to point out a couple of key phases in this text which can help us. The words "so that" show the relationship between God's comfort of *US* in our affliction, and our call to comfort others.

Have you ever felt God's comfort during a difficult time in your life? It's a pretty amazing thing, isn't it? Of course, he comforts us because he loves us and we're his children. But he also comforts us *SO THAT* we may be able to comfort others. He has shown us the way through his own example.

For years, I have understood this passage to mean that, at a minimum, God could use my trial to help another person somewhere down the road who was going through the same thing. Now that I'm a widow, I can be a comfort to other widows.

But if we look more closely, we see that it doesn't say, "…so that we can comfort those who are in the same boat as us." It says, comfort those who are in *ANY AFFLICTION*. Any affliction! That's pretty all-encompassing, isn't it?

So essentially, it's telling us that if we've ever experienced God's comfort through our trial, we are now equipped to comfort others no matter *WHAT* they are going through.

It's been said that God doesn't comfort us to make us comfortable; he comforts us to make us comforters.

Do you see how these scripture verses emphasize the importance of God's people taking up the mantle of compassion? But just because we think it's a great idea, doesn't mean we feel equipped to do it.

You may be thinking to yourself, "I'm still not good at this. This still isn't my gift."

Understanding the importance of being compassionate is just one piece of this picture. The other piece is understanding how God can work through us.

Because when he so clearly calls us to this,

do we really think he won't equip us for it?

But just how does that happen?

I mentioned the secret weapon at the beginning of the appendix and, if you're a believer, it really isn't so secret. It's the power of the Holy Spirit living within us. I've understood for years that when someone becomes a Christian, God's Spirit indwells us. But it's only been in the last few years that I've begun to grasp the depth of power available through this Holy Spirit.

There are *MANY* roles that the Holy Spirit fills in our lives, but I just want to focus now on the fruits of the Spirit. Love, Joy, Peace, Patience, Kindness, Goodness, Faithfulness, Gentleness and Self-Control.

I think you could make a case for every single one of these fruits being helpful in our quest to be compassionate. What would it mean for your outreach to the hurting if you could have an abundance of every single one of these characteristics? Wouldn't you feel like you'd just hit the compassion jackpot?!

Well, here's the simple, but amazing news. When you have the Holy Spirit living within you, you *HAVE* every single one of these characteristics. We just fail to tap into them – or allow the Spirit to work through us.

So, I challenge you to examine your thinking on this if it's a new concept to you. Rather than feeling like you don't have any of the characteristics necessary to step into someone's pain, *ASK* God to empower you through these fruits of the Spirit. It's not *OUR* abilities that will make us successful in this, it's God and his Spirit working through us.

Still don't feel equipped for that mission? Here's what God said to the Apostle Paul in 2 Corinthians 12:9 about that:

> *"My grace is sufficient for you, for my*
> *power is made perfect in weakness."*
> *Therefore I will boast all the more gladly*
> *of my weaknesses, so that the power*
> *of Christ may rest upon me.*

So, in total, all these scriptures and exhortations become your biblical motivation for stepping into your friend's hurting world. Because God's Word commands it, and models it — and because God will be faithful and equip you for it.

It's my prayer that this will give you a glimmer of hope that you can, with God's help, be that compassionate friend.

Appendix B

God Works Through Our Trials

If you've lived any number of years on this earth, chances are high you've had some experience with trials. The length and depth and frequency of them is most likely out of your control (although our life choices *DO* bring some extra ones our way).

But as a general rule, God is in charge of the trials that appear in our lives.

I'd like to begin with a statement that has become one of the mainstays in my life: **God does his best and most permanent work through our trials**.

Have you ever considered how much of creation models for us the many ways that God works *THROUGH* our trials? Should we really be surprised by that? What can we learn from that? And can it give us any comfort?

Consider just a sampling of the ways a struggle is essential for growth in nature. Some of those may be well-known to you; others may be new food for thought.

- The emperor moth must struggle to break free from the cocoon that has encased it during its infancy *SO THAT* its wings become strong enough to allow it to soar. Man's attempt at "freeing" the poor thing by widening the cocoon opening results in... death.

- When the eagle wants to rise above a storm quickly, it uses the raging storm to lift it above the clouds. This eventually gives the eagle an opportunity to glide and rest its wings. It *USES* the storm to reach calmer skies.

- Any good gardener knows that one of the very best ways to coax additional growth from plants is to prune them. Take out the dead, unproductive parts. Sometimes it seems almost cruel to the plant! But the end result is more fruit, more growth, and more productivity. More of what the plant was intended for!

- Often, after some of the destructive forces we mentioned above, we are amazed at how quickly green growth appears. What seemed like utter destruction resulted in a new beginning.

- There is some disagreement among

scientists as to the effect of storms on a tree's root system. So, I will refrain from camping out on that phenomenon, even if there is some truth to it. But, what they *DO* seem to agree on is that strong winds, in conjunction with a tree's ability to *SWAY* with that wind, absolutely create a stronger trunk system. The trees that are *MOST* protected in a forest are often the weakest.

We don't have to use much of our imaginations to see some strong ties between the storms and struggles of nature and our OWN trials. Shouldn't that give us some degree of comfort? At the very least, it should cause us to realize that a trial is absolutely part of the process of growing. And if we put our complete trust in the "Pruner," we too can soar higher, produce more fruit and develop a fortitude that we would not see without the trial.

I'm not saying your trials are any kind of picnic. They aren't. I certainly wouldn't wish the pain of losing my husband on anyone – at least not without the growth. But since you will have trials in this life, I do pray that you can look through that trial, even through your tears, to the result that our loving God has intended for you.

Look for the blessing through the storm. I promise you it's there. Even if it's just in the knowledge that God walked through it with you, and brought you out of it.

I want to share with you a slightly unorthodox way of looking at scripture, specifically texts that talk about how God comforts us through our trials. But I want you to read through these as if they were a series of paragraphs, *WITHOUT* the actual scripture references. [The references are footnoted at the end of this appendix.]

I found that reading all of these straight through without stopping to cite the reference makes the impact extremely powerful. So let the truth of these words wash over you and give you peace and comfort and assurance, no matter what you're going through today.

Blessed is the man who remains steadfast under trial, for when he has stood the test he will receive the crown of life, which God has promised to those who love him.[1] And after you have suffered a little while, the God of all grace, who has called you to his eternal glory in Christ, will himself restore, confirm, strengthen, and establish you.[2]

I have said these things to you, that in me you may have peace. In the world you will have tribulation. But take heart; I have overcome the world.³ Count it all joy, my brothers, when you meet trials of various kinds, for you know that the testing of your faith produces steadfastness.⁴

Not only that, but we rejoice in our sufferings, knowing that suffering produces endurance, and endurance produces character, and character produces hope…⁵ Beloved, do not be surprised at the fiery trial when it comes upon you to test you, as though something strange were happening to you. But rejoice insofar as you share Christ's sufferings, that you may also rejoice and be glad when his glory is revealed.⁶

For I consider that the sufferings of this present time are not worth comparing with the glory that is to be revealed to us.⁷ In this you rejoice, though now for a little while, if necessary, you have been grieved by various trials, so that the tested genuineness of your faith— more precious than gold that perishes though it is tested by fire—may be found to result in praise and glory and honor at the revelation of Jesus Christ.⁸

So we do not lose heart. Though our outer self is wasting away, our inner self is being renewed day by day. For this light momentary affliction is preparing for us an eternal weight of glory beyond all comparison.[9]

I hope you felt like you were just wrapped up in a warm blanket! Our great God *IS* a God of comfort and his Word reminds us of that again and again. In that, we rejoice…

---

[1] James 1:12

[2] 1 Peter 5:10

[3] John 16:33

[4] James 1:2-3

[5] Romans 5:3-4

[6] 1 Peter 4:12-13

[7] Romans 8:18

[8] 1 Peter 1:6-7

[9] 2 Corinthians 4:16-17

About the Author

Lynne Hoeksema

Lynne Hoeksema is a grateful product of the Midwest. She spent her professional career in the corporate world for more than 20 years before choosing to retire early to spend more time with her husband, Dale, who was 20 years her senior. She has a degree in Statistics from Iowa State University and an MBA from Drake University. However, none of that background adequately prepared her for the topic of this book.

That journey began on October 16, 2017 when her husband passed away unexpectedly, and she was thrown into the world of widowhood. But that event alone did not equip her for this subject. During the weeks and months after her husband's death, she saw many friends struggling to know what to say to her, or how to be a comfort.

Having spent years on *THAT* side of grieving and struggling with those same fears herself, she now has a new perspective — one that eventually led to a ministry entitled, *Be a Blessing to Your Grieving Friend*.

She speaks and writes through her ministry site to educate and enlighten her readers. She also writes a personal blog, *It's Beyond Me*, which chronicles insights and lessons through this season of grief.

When she's not writing, you can find Lynne hanging out with her fur children, Daisy, Winnie and Max, the cat (not pictured) or behind the piano at her church or local care facility, or at choir practice with a great group of middle and high schoolers preparing for the next big concert.

About the Ministry

Be a Blessing to Your Grieving Friend

When you marry someone 20 years older, the chances of being a younger widow are pretty high. And I had often wondered what God might have for me someday when I was alone. I thought it might be related to one or two of my passions — maybe music, maybe dogs. Maybe singing dogs? But, oh no, the ministry God would call me to would be the direct result of my husband's death and the pain associated with that.

Like many widows, I witnessed friends struggling with how to interact with me during this season. Clearly, it was uncomfortable for them and the distance resulting from that discomfort was painful for me. But eventually I was reminded that I, too, had struggled with that same awkwardness.

But now, on *THIS* side of my deep loss, I see things differently. I can now tell you from personal experience which words and actions are helpful, and which are not. God began to instill in me a passion to share this new-found wisdom with the friends of those who are hurting, so they can ultimately be the blessing so desperately needed.

From that small seed, the *"Be a Blessing to Your Grieving Friend"* ministry was born. What followed was an educational-based website designed to provide practical advice and perspectives to equip the comforter.

And to be clear, the principles can apply to nearly any type of loss – not just loss from death. Divorce, job loss, chronic illness, disability and virtually any way we can suffer in this fallen world can all be categorized as "loss."

While I pray everyone will benefit from what I share through this speaking/writing ministry, I also speak directly to believers, challenging you to understand what scripture says about showing compassion, and learning how God, through his Holy Spirit, can equip you for that mission.

So, whether it be through this book, a blog post, a speaking engagement, a radio interview, or an impromptu one-on-one chat with a friend, my prayer is that God would work through me to share his wisdom for cultivating compassion.

To learn more about this ministry, please visit my ministry website. Or you can find personal insights into this season of grief by visiting my personal blog, *It's Beyond Me*. I'd be honored if you would share this book, or any of my blog posts with those you love.

Thank you for joining me on this journey.

lynnehoeksema.com
itsbeyondme.blog

THANK YOU!

Compassion in Action

30-60-90 Day Plan

Thank you for reading *Cultivating Compassion!* Are you unsure what to do next? Do you wish you had some guidelines to put the knowledge you've gained into action?

Then, download this FREE PDF designed to do just that! It will help:

- *Identify those in your life who need your compassion*
- *Decide what are the best ways to reach out to them*
- *Guide you through the scheduling and follow-up process*
- *Provide sample conversations when words fail you*

Grab your **FREE** copy here:

lynnehoeksema.com/compassion-in-action/

Published Author of
Cultivating Compassion
Practical Advice as You Walk a Friend
through a Season of Loss
Lynne Hoeksema

BOOK LYNNE TO SPEAK

Lynne is available to be your keynote
speaker or your workshop leader.

Lynne speaks openly about what she experienced after the death of
her husband of 31 years. Her ministry and her desire is to help you
navigate the tricky waters of walking through grief with others.
Her "behind the scenes" perspective and practical knowledge
will give you the confidence to step out in faith
and bless someone in their time of need.

*"I certainly didn't expect what
I heard to touch my heart to
the depth it did. Everything
I have done before was
turned upside down. What
I learned will help me serve
others much more effectively."*

*"Lynne told us things that we
don't want to ask, but need
to know."*

*"Thank you for reminding us
that we don't always need to
have the right words. Just be
there and listen."*

BE A BLESSING
TO YOUR GRIEVING FRIEND

lynne@lynnehoeksema.com
itsbeyondme.blog
lynnehoeksema.com/speaking

CAN YOU HELP?

Hey, thanks for reading
Cultivating Compassion!

If you could spare just a few minutes,
I'd appreciate your honest review
on Amazon.com.
Just search for my book
and leave a brief review.

THANK YOU!